D0462008

OUT TO DRY IN CAPE BRETON

DISCARDED.

Out to Dry
in Cape Breton

Anita Lahey

Nanton Thelma Fanning Library
Box 310
Nanton, Alberta T0L 1R0

Signal
EDITIONS

SIGNAL EDITIONS IS AN IMPRINT OF VÉHICULE PRESS

Published with the generous assistance of The Canada Council for the Arts and the Book Publishing Industry Development Program of the Department of Canadian Heritage.

Signal Editions editor: Carmine Starnino

Cover design: David Drummond
Photo of author: Mark Sutcliffe
Set in Minion by Simon Garamond
Printed by Marquis Book Printing Inc.

Copyright © Anita Lahey 2006
All rights reserved.

Library and Archives Canada Cataloguing in Publication Data

Lahey, Anita
Out to dry in Cape Breton / Anita Lahey
Poems.
ISBN 1-55065-209-5
1. Cape Breton Island (N.S.)—Poetry. I. Title.

PS8623.A393O88 2006   C811'.6   C2005-907144-3

Published by Véhicule Press, Montréal, Québec, Canada
www.vehiculepress.com

Distribution in Canada by LitDistCo
orders@litdistco.ca
Distributed in the U.S. by Independent Publishers Group
www.ipgbook.com

Printed in Canada

for
Joana Fraser (1971-1994)
who led me to poems

and
Diana Brebner (1956-2001)
who led me back again

Acknowledgements

I extend my thanks to the editors (in some cases former editors) of the following publications, where many of these poems previously appeared: *The Antigonish Review, Arc, The Fiddlehead, The Malahat Review, The New Quarterly, Pagitica* and *This Magazine*. Several poems here were first published in the anthologies *Breathing Fire 2: Canada's New Poets,* and *The New Canon: An Anthology of Canadian Poetry*. "Post-war Procession" first appeared in the pantoum chapter of *In Fine Form: The Canadian Book of Form Poetry*. "Billboard Girl" first appeared on buses in Ottawa, as part of Transpoetry.

"Out to Dry in Cape Breton" won *The Fiddlehead's* Ralph Gustafson Prize for Best Poem, 2003. An excerpt from "Cape Breton Relative" won *The Antigonish Review's* Great Blue Heron Poetry Contest, 2004. Groups of poems in this manuscript were shortlisted for *The Malahat Review* Long Poem Prize and also earned first honourable mention in the Bronwen Wallace Award for Poetry. My sincere thanks to the judges and organizers of these competitions.

I am grateful to the Canada Council for the Arts, which provided financial assistance for writing, and to the Banff Centre for the Arts Wired Writing program.

This book would not exist without the members of the Gang of Four—Lesley Buxton, Dilys Leman and Una McDonnell—whom I thank with deep appreciation for fearless and unwavering (and often entertaining) critique. Also John Barton, Stephanie Bolster and the late Diana Brebner, for their astonishingly generous mentorship and friendship. I thank Sue Goyette for opening my ear to rhythm, and my editor, Carmine Starnino, for helping me see things large and small. My most heartfelt gratitude to my father, who gave me permission to mine his world; to my mother, for lifelong guidance and encouragement; and to Mark Sutcliffe, for support of all kinds.

Contents

CAPE BRETON RELATIVE

WOMAN AT CLOTHES LINE

WOMAN AT CLOTHES LINE

Strapped sandals lift the lady
above the lawn. Hung linens adopt her
hippy contours. This is no steamy

Tide commercial. Our star is absorbed
in cooler, wetter realities. She wears
a blue dress, white scarf. Her mouth

twitches wryly into some future. What
rustles toward her through the October
yard? Consider recklessness, how it breeds

in safe places. Was laundry ever just
a chore? Hold a rinsed blouse to your
face. Gaze through its weave at the gauzy

world. Notice how whiteness drinks itself
blue, agitates the fallen red
leaves. Those blankets have been under

your skin; they have things to tell you—
grey, woolly things. She lugs them out
to air their moth-eaten souls. How

gracefully she hoists her basket, all her
disappointments. It's clear from her eyes, the absence
of pins. Nothing here will blow away.

WASH WITH A VIEW

Wash clings to yawning lines,
shivering damp. Corners

bend like pages you'll go back to. Hems
buckle beneath this gaunt Yorkshire

sky. A cough of chilled air
sends your line downhill, to Halifax. Dishevelled,
it drapes soot-stained rooftops

in want: more, this time, than a soak
and a twist. Potato-bag shirts, string-bean
bras. All scatter toward the precipice—

snatched in time by the diligent

plastic pins, red and yellow (shades
of emergency intervention). New stains
are never far off. Blossoms brush

mustard on stockings, slips, hints
at who would win, if it came to that.
Spin, dry, fold. Tuck into tissue-

lined drawers. What is this endless
procession? I hang my clothes

on a solitary line that leans toward no ledge. One

peg, two hems, security in pairs. Yet
they cower, absorbing fumes. Purple thistle
creeps, claws stiff jaundiced threads.

There is little comfort in that.

THE DRIP-DRY METHOD

An airy kiss, our fabrics come
alive. Face cloths wring

dances from laden rope. Your
grey-haired jeans yee-ha
over green tomatoes. We hunker

indoors, wondering how to begin
our own jig—when, for God's sake,
here will be enough. Tie up

the hollyhocks, prostrate, breaking
their backs. Pick the peppers, fold the clothes.
Weeds writhe beneath the morning

glory, overgrown and slithering
through the back door. Can't we spare
a wooden peg to fasten our promise

to that line? Please. It is you
I have chosen. Keep me

hinged, assure me of this patched rug
we've laid down, which fades daily
in ways I don't understand. What we do

for love. I would gladly be wrung, hung—
bash myself against walls

of humid air. We need an honest
soaking, then the pegs, the windy harvest
dance—you and I wrestling with all that

ripens and blows between our seams.

THINGS THAT MIGHT PREVENT YOU
FROM HANGING

the clothes out to dry: sore arms. A shortage
of pegs. High winds. Underwear trimmed
with lace. A snapped line. That feeling of unease

that arises when you see acrylic sleeves (yesterday
they held your own arms) emaciated, unable
to contain their nervousness. Mud. An absence

of nostalgia in your veins. You are shy and under
five feet. Tattered underwear, waistbands drawling. Bylaws
that forbid colourful displays of household chores. Fear

of stiff joints. Fatigue. Nightmares of being
dismembered. An addiction to the feathery smell
of fabric softener. Airborne pollution (orange, clinging

to cotton). Drizzle. Some misunderstanding with Sabine,
your cat. Lightning. Laziness (an automatic dryer
in the basement). Age. A lost button. You believe

in the roundness of the planet but don't
trust it. The Wham! decal on that t-shirt you wear
only beneath other clothes. Freezing rain. Nightmares

about boys stealing your clothes off a rock
while you swim in the limestone quarry
at Hagersville. Sunburn. An unwillingness

to venture outdoors: You are nude, all your clothing
in the wash. A broken pulley. Squirrels. An inability to appreciate
old-fashioned labour. You eat corn chips and salsa

on Mondays. You hate to see the faithful upended in one long row,
fluids rushing, airheads pounding. It makes you want to cry.

A WOMAN TO HER ABDOMEN,
HANGING ON THE LINE

Go on smirking, whitish bulge. Insist
on your turn in the sun. No blast
of wind will diminish your proud

arc, loping curves, inviting
indentations. Go on: Store my
hunger, chew my pain. Must you

demand to be filled with sweets,
proteins, love? Some Tuesday night
you may gurgle, whip up

new life. Did I ask for your tricks,
slippery folds? All that pinching
under belts, the softest gowns? God

how you bloat, you meddler,
nag. I prefer to be hollow
from the waist down. Let washer-women

trample my sack, lye pinking thighs,
songs ripping guts till nothing
remains save flesh battered

free of soils, pockets of fat. While dripping
dry, keep your belching
to yourself. I will turn you

out as I wish, fold you flat as sheets.

THREE BATH MATS SUSPENDED

Clap-clap puckered rubber over
Hintonburg shed: close mouth, open
mouth, gulp first light, rise

to dew. Pebble-stuccoed walls, disembowelled
oven in the lot. She's bright-eyed but still
yawning, up since six, that ember

drawing lines along her face. The kids
thank God in bed. It's between her
and that steeple with its silver cap, hands

on its hips, dressing her yard up
in clangs, ding-dongs. As if more racket
will help. She goes for the eyes

with emerald, navy, peacock
blue—a lush trio teasing
clouds, garnishing corrugated

rust. They ought to splatter
all over God's concrete

steps, but they're made too well, don't
approve of disarray. We all have one
blessing we can't afford. Hers is

colour, erupting hard as bells. Douse
that butt, feed the kids, haul your bones

through one more morning. Show
that prissy steeple how you squeeze
blue glory from sidewalks, ta-dah. Drink

me, do it now, before the day
blinks, and brilliance melts away.

WASH DAY IN A TORONTO SLUM

You in the buggy squirming your baby
fat out from under the belt, you'll one day
be a mama with your own splitting

pegs and twelve charges, scoured black
and white shrouds that kick earth won't
bother coming clean, what for? And the health

inspector will pace with his photographer, blank
don't-notice-you're-Black expression, and you
will tell him Look, lookit me, I survived

this survival you see hanging here
looking so sorry—what it seems it isn't.
Here: patched rear ends, mended

pockets—keep your hands
outta! Pencil nudging his ear he'll finger
your stockings (writhing), absorb

those dresses wrung to pallor. All he need
do is peer behind (he might as well). There
dangle flowers, locks of hair, flour-caked

aprons and a soggy Bible flapping: life
splayed for inspection. What's the use? He'll

just note that muddy unpaid
bill, Grandpa's tea-brown teeth, heels
grown through old shoes—and germs:

dancing, multiplying . . . And he'll signal
Mr. Sidekick (snap the photo, flash
this horror) with your daughter

gripping the stroller you scrambled
from too young: she's digging her nails in, wishing
to spit and you will remember, must

remember tearing at the clotheslines, yanking
holy laundry in a heap shouting *How else
will the clothes dry?* Out back tempting

filth and damnation, where pink-petal noses
inhale their one-cent bruises. You will be a mama,
a grandma, baby fat long toiled off and still

inspectors will (not bother to) knock, recoil
at your lack of closets, discretion, punish you
for wringing squalor out, forcing them to watch

it rock and sway like any leaf or dandelion
seed or sunlit particle of dust, thing of beauty.

THE SILVER BUGGY HANDBOOK

Assembly

Gather burnished silver
spoons, chrome fixtures and the proud
reflective frames of torn

vinyl chairs. Melt, stir, pour
into hard steel strips. Weld
to form a shimmering

basket on wheels. Fill with milk,
turkey and gooey-nosed children
who whack at rows of soup cans
and demand to be driven home.

Care

The buggy is a low rider; it rears, snorts, begs
to shine like the hubcaps on Jimmy's Corvette.

Polish daily. Rub spokes, into mirrors
too narrow to reflect a cheekbone. Consider
light, entwined in the rough
grid of a shopping cart.

Riding

When your older brother (protector,
menace) races you through
cereal to dairy to pasta, remember:
elbows in, heels down, fingers

hooked like claws. Bars blur
to grey streaks as you
speed through frozen foods.

Driving

Before backing out remove debris. Fliers
flaunt chicken at two-ninety-nine
a pound. Rotting greens and mulching

newsprint tarnish your silvery net. Go
fish. Aisle one. Resist slouching
over handlebars. Round corners

gingerly, on all fours. If the front
left wheel sticks, let it. Absorb

the skid. Reverse without malice
if parked between the widower and his cat
food, the stock broker and her
low-fat ravioli.

Packing

Bread belongs in the baby
seat, the safest place for
soft, precious things. Turn
the lime plastic seat up

or down, as you wish. Shove
potatoes in their tough bags
on the bottom rack. Layer
the rest: meat first, fruit last. Behold

sustenance in its grim
metal cage in the supermarket
glare. Do not sneak biscuits from bright
yellow boxes with sharp corners.

Living

Keep blankets and clothes in bags
that bulge through wires dull

with rust. Stack tattered
books, chipped mug, your favourite
cap. Black garbage bag
for rain, the green bottle. Which
are you most likely to need

in a moment of panic? Hunch low
on bustling thoroughfares, but race
the sweet back alleys. Dodge broken glass.

THE USUAL SPIN

Every life contains a wheel
to treasure, fear, pursue. It hotdogs
down the road. Roll,
dizzy, roll. Fling pop-a-

wheelie. Where on the hill
will you land? Wheels you love

with rags, a bitter cream. Wheels
slip-sliding beneath eager feet.
The wheel that deflates when you turn

away. Your brothers think the way out
is by the wheel—four of them, cornered,
at the mercy of ruts and nails. You at the table

twisting coins into dervishes, trapping
fevers with your thumb. Believe the somersaulting
in your chest, lifeblood in rollicking

vessels. There are hubs you won't stop
going back to. Water, Ferris, cheese. Wheels
you spin because you can. In the old black Ford

you will slouch before a beige circular
leather, lower your eyes, and laugh. Fists

at ten and two, that gravel crunch
between rim and road, hiccup of sky

half a revolution away. Time is the oldest
tire, balding from overuse, unconcerned
with potholes, forward, reverse—insistent

earth tugging it down, shoving it along.

THE ELEMENT OF CARRYING ON

The wind doesn't know what it wants
anymore than we do. It grabs what it can
and blasts its way through mortar, barrels
down the chimney. Some days it saunters up
and unhinges the door. Now the wind
is walled in with you and me and the dust and the three
model boats, red and built by a guy named Keeping. It lies
heaving like an old hound on the carpet, giving off
mustiness, sweat. The wind dreams of hunting, kicking
its weary legs. It too can swim. All of us try to remember
where we've been, the things that were so important
to see and do. How many foreheads flattened
against the glass, turning to the cluttered room
and then, confused, back out to the bay? We look for
the desperation that once propelled us over mountains.
Five, eighteen, twenty-four hours away, thousands
plunk into blue seats on runways, wait to be flown
into prevailing winds, away from those places
they happen to be. Some days I am among them, or
wish I was. I would give up barely holding
ground against the gale: lodge myself in its yowling
maw, snap off calmly in the din. But I keep coming back
to these boats that aren't boats, to you and our rising
mounds of curled-up air that once commanded
wild dogs and oceans, and shaped the pliable trunks of trees.

HARBOUR FLAGS

The Atlantic Ocean whines, coating
her trinkets in drowning
weeds. Bandaged boats chortle
her spine, floundering. Mrs. Wadden's

daisy sheets wave a jaunty
farewell. She presses linen to reddened
cheeks, eyes bobbing, sterns sketching

wakes of splayed hands: Ease
this antsy harbour. Mrs. Wadden knows

better than to pause after hanging
the wash, familiar panic
rising, boats gliding to fingertips,

breezes humming threats. The weather
will shift, steel-core clothesline jolt:
faded petals tear from her

fists. She may cry, *No! Please! Not today.* Would you
hear her, over the roar? Grasp, fumble,
weigh the line down. What else
can she do? Believe this green plastic was made
to withstand two hundred kilograms. Of what?
Wet wool underwear. Discarded

salt. The bloated dead. This is
what Vesty needed, a heavy-duty
line flung from the shore, pillowcase
fastened to its end. If, if.
She will find him in that cold

cavorting with Irish convicts'
bones, which have turned centuries
in a crone's restless veins. The shipwrecked
can't resist revenge on mothers

who hang bed sheets like bleached
screams. Leave the linen raging, fling
open the washer. The churning
drills her nostrils, batters

each eye. He was a boy. Couldn't
swim. Lonely current now tunnelling, expecting
playmates. A brother, someone's
leftover son.

OUT TO DRY IN CAPE BRETON

Nan hesitates at the window, fingering
lace, humming her quiet history, cut-off
breast. She stares down the old grey

laundry line out back, up the hill, swinging
low. Strong as ever. No use for a body
living on memories and bingo, sweetened

Carnation's in her tea. "Can't get up
there no more," she says. The dryer
crackles; crocheted slippers lose themselves

over and over, drones in a cyclone.
Her bones fret in their thin socks,
waiting. I take the camera with me. My eyes

disrobe the island, gathering bodiless
material: hungry sleeves at White Point,
leggy denim flirting with daisies

by a Louisbourg B&B. She's dying,
I implore. Be still. Whispers slip
through buttonholes, hems. In Albert's Bridge

bath towels drop their pink jaws, trees
lean in to feel tenderness seep into
fog. A local asks, of me, my camera: "You

don't have clotheslines in Ontario?" Damn
mist on the lens. Some things take days
to dry. Nan's tea-stained nightie, sock feet

on torn linoleum, milky breath on glass—
all that dampness dreaming static. The line
out back, sighing, tied fast to its posts.

DISREPAIR

Canopy clothesline in the yard, weeping,
abandoned web
faltering like arms of old
men for whom weightlessness is a burden.

Woman, poised, wet mounds in a basket, lips
taut enough to hold
the trunks and towels,
cotton jumpsuits that keep wading into the lake.

Man in the lawn chair, Styrofoam drink
holder squeaking, big toe
tracing crevices in the patio:
circling, rubbing. Young weeds

at every turn. Girl on her back, listening,
inspecting the sky,
maple biceps
under bags of rain. Her mother sighs, bends. Another

yellow towel rises, unfurling
promises, chlorine
dampness encircling
the neck. Matted terry cloth toes brittle grass.

SINKING QUILTS

Everyday rags and wraps forge
a checkered path through the backyard
sky: one long accidental quilt grunting
its way to the monster fir. Rug fringes
tease like hair that skirts your cap. See
her cigarette burn on peppermint
cloth. My father's syrup, sticky
brown warts on that placemat: He noticed
nothing, French toast filling his mouth. I studied them

hard. Three decades of marriage should
tell us what to expect if we let ourselves
grow together one more time. I didn't like
what I saw. Shot looks. Absence of touch. Her
blaming him. What sort of specimens
are they? April births with cyclone
tendencies. We are children of opposing
seasons; winter and summer need
each other for relief. On good days

we call ourselves a team: Simmering
layers prepared by four colliding hands lie
concealed behind that tea towel—peaks
of shepherd's pie, oven-window grease.
Pillowcases pocket air, moon shadows where
our heads would rest did we not inch
inward through the night, fitting grooves.

I claim that pea-pod sheet, a flying cape
to whisk me through the years. We have lost so many
to red-wine and olive-oil stains. Now I am old
enough: I know. It was never Mother's fault. Air
leaves a crust on spun jeans. The quilt peels off

the sky in pieces. What we use most,
cherish, neatly hung, barely gets off the ground.

WHY YOUR WHITE TUBE SOCKS ARE HOLEY

You choose which side
covers the heel, always
the same, humming, unrolling

their ribbed necks along your calves
before you run: out the door, down
the porch the walk the road the path that takes you
away from my loving grip. These brief,

sweaty escapes. If only you'd come back
with songs and famished lips. I button

my expectations quietly over your chest. You know
what I like: blues and Billie Holiday, your voice
let loose, wrung socks on the line

squirming to hear. Hold still. Let the music
run through your shredding heels. Listen
for when you don't need me. Your ballads, your

filling me partly: all that is rundown, trailing
off-key. Thank God you know how to

sing, shut me up, close
my eyes as you touch
your voice to the sky.

LATE FOR THE GAME

Two-thousand five-hundred and twenty
games in Cal Ripken's streak: Call it

commitment, a guy who's lost if not
at third base. We are here to observe. But

we've missed the stop at Camden Yards, crossed
oily water on a thin rail, left the heroes

of Baltimore behind. The tram brakes, doors
slide open to cracked-up lots, siding

all battered, chipped. Have we been led
to some answer? Just another dreary

scene. At the fourth house, a ketchup-red
jersey hangs out, teasing that dress with blue

arms thrown down in defeat. Imagine

a girl, stealing third, in the dirt, skirt
at her hips. The sky is full of running

streaks. Who knows when to let go? I peruse
the local technique: swing each garment

in the soupy air. Never overlap decaying
seams. We ought to leave something out

on the line: My hawk-eyed reading of signals; your need
for a rising score. Me off the bag, taunting; you

in the hole, open-gloved, one dusty
eye holding me in place.

I HAVE CHOSEN LOVE

Somewhere a version of me is not
allowing herself to be ushered

through breathless hotels on puff
flour beaches where maids turn down the bed

depositing squares of chocolate, and you
dish buffets of simmering basil affection.

I should know where she is, what
unclean surfaces massage her

behind, how her tongue maneouvres, licking
contours of unfamiliar sounds—

what it is to suffer
the absence of you. I

have chosen the fear of unraveling
limbs, this fragile bliss,

its threats of decay. So we are dared
to love. So what? What could rival

the sway of her—rootless, bare, gorging
on lava air? She marches into pungent

Andean marketplaces by herself, no
broad hand nudging the small of her

back, brushing a cheek goodbye, cradling
whispers: what time later to meet, to feel

whole. I left her that day you convinced me
to run for the train, your whistling

skin at the far end of the track. I return
to haunt her, feel her prowling

that shadowed room: window on the alley, damp
laundry on chair backs. What might she confide

about the bruised, stoic soul? She craves
volcanoes and falling skies, laughs and opens

wide, wider—gulping words I never, swaddled
in purple-leaf joy, will taste. Could she endure

a single tucked-in night? Lure you
with sugarcane fingers through mangrove

swamps? I would welcome, you know, some horror:
fall bawling into grit, watch oozing

knees unwrap—no borrowed fingers
to meld within my clutching fear. One timid

knock, oh send me
hurtling (don't!)

to myself. Suppose
she doesn't know me. Suppose she does.

SUSPENSION

Outside Isabela, Puerto Rico

Into this sun-bleached universe
we blink: which way
to direct our rented car? This morning
you swam the sea and I
some sky, atop a mild horse, daydreaming
of see-through waves and neon fins. We rose early
due to life's roaring, ocean horn blasting
salt in our pores. Might we linger
here, with polished stone
fragments between toe skins? No. The day

bugles: wade deeper, yet again, one
body to another, another. Tumble
through citrus archways, gesturing
palms, clouds of courtyard doves. We should
stop, look back, look long. Behind
sherbet-orange pickets, Puerto Ricans suspend
t-shirts by the waist before disintegrating
stucco. In clothes-pinned shadows they miss

nothing, as we pass, and pass again. How we
kick, paddle, strive. A foot may slip, lung
collapse under too much brine, and that will be
all. It may prove too much, or not
enough. We went with motion, so we
move. Watch my fingers fondle the textures
of home, familiar weight of laundry, settling down.

Post-war Procession

POST-WAR PROCESSION

After *Infantry, near Nijmegen, Holland*, 1946,
Alex Colville, oil on canvas

Envy the barrel's ability to contain nothing.
You stink of blood, a blown-open field, severed
limbs. The march in was less pungent. Puddles, open
wounds along the ditch. Your rifle cools your neck.

You stink of blood, a blown-open field. Severed,
still following orders, boots, the men in front,
wounds along the ditch. Your rifle, your neck,
yellow leak of sky. Bodies reek in your head.

Still following orders. The boots of men in front
reflect your own: polished, tightly tied.
That yellow leak of sky. Bodies reek. Your head
inside the helmet; gripping your skull.

Reflect. Your own polished, tightly tied
meltdown. Mud. This endless trudge
inside the helmet gripping your skull.
The march continues. On the other side:

meltdown, mud, this endless trudge—
hands unfolding letters you barely wrote.
The march continues on the other side.
The horizon claws you back with white fingers

unfolding. Letters you barely wrote,
wishing your work was done. Forget glory being alive.
The horizon claws you back; its white fingers
draw out your every accomplishment, ghastly

wish. Your work is done. Forget glory: being alive
is the long walk you knew it would be.
Draw out your every ghastly accomplishment.
Envy the barrel's ability. Contain nothing.

WOMEN'S WORK, AFTER VE DAY

After *Canteen, Nijmegen Holland*, 1945, Molly Lamb Bobak,
oil and ink on canvas

I am dispatched: the canteen
my only battleground. I paint it
like any other. Here, a girl

in a knotted brown tie. Collar
smart, sleeves rolled, she prepares
to balance the final course

on her right hand. So much lies
in her favour: eggshell skin, unblemished;
elfin ears, intact. A circular tray

stocked with cupcakes, éclairs, served
by her on the rationed front, night
upon night—gifts passed in dreams

to the fallen. I usher her into lamp-lit
afternoon, hushed revelations:

Chelmno, Belsen, Buchenwald. Pit
after foul pit. The future crusts like icing
on a half-risen Bundt. She concentrates

on stuck berries, layers of cream, her arm
in that muscular pause before swirling the tray
above her head. Something spices the canteen

air, their perfect ties, discreet exchanges—

impossible to light up, brush down. Every vile
feast is followed by cake, white cake
a girl in uniform will be ordered to carry. And she will.

IN THE BUILDING OF FUTURE EXPLOSIONS

After *Women Making Shells*, 1919, Mabel May, oil on canvas

Some women don't knit socks or bundle
sterile rolls of cloth. They impale their thighs

with giant silver bullets in their sleep.
Green lamps cast cones of light, the light

of ages: wizened, deceptively weak. Colours
of melancholy, sleeves. Wheels crank, ropes

lash, arguing distantly. All hair pinned and
capped. This mother, that wife. Wide-eyed

sweethearts armed with little bombs. A redhead
grips metal, nose down. Instructing the shell

who not to kill. One faceless woman

heaves a finished weapon off the pile. It lengthens her,
folds her in two. She bulges with this one

death, wound hard into steel. When
is she to be destroyed? Rafters brace

under banished untolds. Sweat-greased bodies reel
the sons, armed, unarmed, back to the trenched womb.

ARS MORIENDI CREED*

After *Bodies in a Grave, Belsen*, 1946, Alex Colville, oil on canvas

We believe in good death, the drapery
drawn, passing on before morning
unearths all that is known and unknown.

We believe in one body, one grave, the anguished
last thin breath, respectfully consorting
round the news, palm to palm, hush to hush,
wet cheek to wet cheek, besotted, afraid, obediently
bending into sorrow. Mythology

pumps through our veins. We decompose
our way to salvation under stones
propped up by the living: we lie
buttoned in velvet dresses grimly
submitting to cavalries of worms, acting
sacred. By whose disregard

are we brutalized one by one? They were
tortured, gassed and buried. On the next day
the conscript arrived undefended and fierce;
he descended into corpse after corpse with his right hand

memorizing horror. He drew four half-rotten
forms into sombre light, and our shame

purples, distends. We believe in the comfort
of skin, fed stomachs, which swell
into hope. The artist's dutiful eye. The ribs
of the ruined protrude and divide. They are broken,

passed around. We believe in one daughter
by every deathbed. We acknowledge her resolve,
the tissue in her fist. We look for shifting
bundles underground, the dead doing what they do.

*in echo of the Nicene Creed

GASPING

Dry faster caplin, until sea dribbles away
all reminder of blessed moisture. Copper

sweat funnels, streaking sinewy bodies—
dying shreds. Trim fish on a line:

each beak-bitten worm writhes alone. Pant
goodbye to sun, cruel air, sharp-haired tails

caught mid-thrash. Your torpedo noses aim
all wrong: What is left to find? No blinking, no diving, no

sign of salvation. As bait, your scales
might have kept that penny shine. Would you

have rustled fins, squawked gills till cod bit?
Mallotus Villosus, it could be worse. This choking

sky paints tides. Trust even dead scales to incise
gummy palms. Revenge, a translucent finger, beckons:

one lash-free, unmoving eye beholds the house,
the other devours the horizon.

[From "Nine Deaths"]

RAPTURE (DEATH SIX)

Counting under shelter at the side
of the house. Kaboom! One, two—

Crack! Two, three. Air weighs
like rough wool on your skin.

Rack-a-juk-a-broondle, four, five, six: Earth bellows

her joy, pretending anger.
Maples raise their soggy arms; the field weeps

its love for the sky. The ground heaves

and sighs: Watch her surrender, and surrender,
till rain recedes, till the miles between roaring
and whitewashed ecstasy count eight, till

you can bare it no more and you sidle
into the cool, slick aftermath of passion. Go barefoot,
the sole being the root of all

honesty. This land, glassy as daybreak,
brims with untapped explosions:
Yodel, I say! Warble. Trill a tremor higher
than a splinter of ice. Jump, kick yourself

open. The clouds split into one
rapturous avenue: light, belting you
over, gathering you in. You fly,

trailing sparks. And lo, you are engulfed.

CONSUMPTION (DEATH THREE)

Hunger is blue ice, a cherry fever
haunting your spine. Train your wanting

down, to the right. Plum shadows
blanket your collarbone, impress the chin, lie

where shadows have no business. Walls
melt as you recede into mottled caverns.

Needle arms hang, fingers threading,
threading. With one yank, your hair

lets go. How to urge breasts toward
faith, quit this slinking

along the ribs? Down cranks the mouth,
cheekbones rise, flushed crags

out of rubble. A blue-brown bruise
hovers, your forehead, waiting

to land. You know your stomach
better than yourself. This is need.

It pulses; bluer than pain, the oldest
sky. It is fruit, fish, a river

refusing to freeze. Your only eye.

ARMILLARIA ROOT DISEASE (DEATH FIVE)

A tree grows choices: the axe, the bolt,
the beetle, the flame. None of these

for you white spruce with your grey
crust, cones of red-lipped scales. Retreat

from the bottom up. Peel your bark against
that Douglas fir exuding prickly health. Creak;

groan. Make your dying heard, make it

slow. Resin bubbles, glues your pores. Microscopic
strands, sticky-white, gum your ancient roots.

The aspen worries its thousand hearts, green
voices fanning, flapping. Mushrooms lie

at your feet. A traveller pauses, hoping
for food, finds green starlight escaping

hardened knots: she takes your branches
for magic wands. You begin to go

bald. The forest sleeps. Now you wear a cold
luminescence in the black-hole dark:

You have swallowed the night. Aah, the slow

death, careening—and later, that long
mulch. Listen: inconsolable roots

release the hostage earth. Hear something
spin, glint, grind its way into light.

SEVEN-FOOT BALSAM FIR FROM
THE PARKDALE MARKET

It takes two to sacrifice a fir. Wear lined
boots, toques. Find a shaggy miser
clinging to greenness. Prepare to starve
its resin-coated heart. Lug your catch down the slush-ridden
road. Audacity's bristled arms flap between you:
heady with plans to stuff the forest through the front
door. Sap congeals on your mitts. Prop the tree on the living-room
floor; stab with silver screws. Think of woods, night, a diet
of snow. Remember bitter afternoons at the cut-your-own,
axe in your dad's gloved hand, Mom clutching a thermos. The studied
circling of branches, winter caking your nose. The severed
tree hauls water up its spine, sheds onto unopened
gifts. Legless, it weeps the sticky-raw scent of why, how, when?

We enter the room as the year recedes. Woodsy sweetness
gathers in prickly heaps. We vacuum, we sweep. We see
what the tree is capable of knowing, unable to know it
ourselves. The rug thickens with our disappearing. Plastic
replicas threaten to rise from the basement: squashed, evergreen,
the opposite of truth. The nose lives for these wintry
thefts, the acrid memory of that stained-glass man. His blood
was not enough. Every year a tree dies in the house, one
thirsted needle at a time. Months later, remnants
thread into socks, jabbing our feet. Unlike
the oak desk, maple floor, Jesus and those six million Jews,
the fir is a fresh kill; we dress it in tinsel, bells. For mercy
we lodge a sliver of sky—an angel, a star—over its uppermost branch.

INSTRUCTIONS ON SNOW

Its canvas, your sky. Watch it wrinkle,
doodle those sugary messages.
Breathe whiteness till it becomes
starlets pinking your throat. Beware
self-important flakes, indigestible

purity, heavenly filaments threading
into ominous blankets. Be a tree.
Be wind.
Shake. Subdue.
There is a six-sided language
we should all learn. This is not about

the blackening heap in the ditch, yellow
sprinkle of dog piss, threat
of acid frost. Do your duty. Stick out
your tongue, that the bleached
world may melt. Snip it from paper

with a steady hand. Suspend the delicate
cold in a window, over the bed.
Haul out your shovels, sleds, well-waxed
skis. Roll the great white into heads
with pocked cheeks, destined to jowl

in the sun. There is snow you plow,
snow you salt. Snow you put on
like a new fleece. Snow you wander into and forget

to leave. Some mornings we wake
under a dreamy layer. Dig in
before the untrod glint retreats: Scoop
mittfuls into your grief, give
to it all your faith in decadence,
ice-cold. Fall. Flatten
and flap, flap till your limbs dissolve.

ABANDONED RAILWAY BRIDGE
OVER THE OTTAWA

Everything is designed to remind us of our smallness. We walk
to prove it doesn't matter, trespass on the CPR line, tromp
into its black-trellised hovering on narrow planks god-knows
how old. Metal arms criss-cross, criss-cross: their taunting,
their gaps. The river tarries beneath puckered skin. There is no alone,
not here. November hurls itself at us, elbows and knees drawn. Pigeons
fuss and coo; clouds stare back; somewhere is a man who fitted rocks
into pillars, laid rails, hammered steel and died. There were men in canoes
who didn't stand a chance. They whisper back and forth. The dead
want peace, but only sometimes. Kids have been here wielding
cans of paint, accusations: *How could you want more than this?* Their uneven
letters lie whitely, backed against flagging sun. A scrubby shore

calls to one you left behind. Midway, the rope, lashed to a jutting
beam. Twenty feet of braided yellow fixed to the sky, fretting
over water. Evidence of swimmers, or worse. Someone climbed
and clung to tie that far-off end. The sky sweeps the river
roughly, without pity. The question is whether to exist in two
places or one. Keep keeping all you've amassed or fling it off
this old bridge. Teeter on rotting boards, tethered by hope.
Or tautly arc into glory and back, glory and back, each triumph
less graspable than the last, until, wind-whipped, with calloused
palms, you yo-yo about, doodling on little sheets of air. In wonder
resides no footing; kicking won't get you home. You're bound
to blackening yellow, nighttime's impressive arrivals, the immoveable
bridge with its slime-plastered legs. Ward off, longly and without
sound, that sweaty, red-palmed slippage as you undulate
with memories of height, the wooden, underfoot sureness that was.

HIGH DIVER

This body, a prayer flung—
steel arch yawning, blue vein
of Earth meandering below, top

down, unprepared for the smack. Me
next, uh-huh, huffed up these girders,
sealed the contract, invisible

phone calls crackling through fields,
iron curling my toes. I crouch. What rises
must fall; you're a message that takes

forever, rosy feet kicking as Earth nurses
your target, one tranquil creek. This
is what you think bridges are for—cute,

country-road spans—not cars or commerce
or even the simpler things (nostalgia,
avoiding soakers). You aim to surprise

the planet, arms awash in gravity, white
bathing suit dripping midday hope. You're
still in mid-dive and the brain works

fast, creek banks crowding my hugged
knees, way up here, so: what if a cramp, your leg, a jerk
to the left? What if a burst of wind?

We are a race of jumpers, little to separate
leaps of glory, despair. I balk at both.
But the telephone poles register your

faith, blinking its quiet sparks—
one, two, three, into the dry-eyed horizon.

And your fingers crash first.
And the impact in your nose, your chest.
And someday you too will hover

at the peak of this arch, before life-
blood, drowned boulders, the possibility of never
fulfilling the pact. Could anyone

escape it? Your bubbling
explodes. And the bridge shrugs its burly shoulder. And I splay.
Earth-breath hot on the soles of my feet.

CONVICTIONS, AT FOURTEEN

I shall do as Mother said: smile, hold
my head like a gift. Keep morbid
notions to myself. Harden

these milk-dud eyes, admitting
nothing. Stop stammering
about bats, beetles, goblins

infesting the garden. Prize unsoiled
stockings. Carry fear like a blanket
on my back. I'll dance, hopefully. Admire

mushrooms, supervise the cook, charm
father's guests with curtsies, untrembling
hands. Practice piano. With the children

I must be saintly, while secretly
drawing terrible pictures. I ought not
slouch, sulk, simper, sigh, linger

at the butcher's, crawl beneath the table, chew
my lip in front of strangers, forget her dying
wishes. Marry. Wear this black dress

again. Perish as daintily as she, ignoring
that withering stench. I plan to shove
my collarbone back where it belongs,

taking the stairs to bed. I might cry
when no one is looking, without knowing
why. I perch on this hard green sofa

fending off light till it sinks through the floor.

NO ONE WATCHING

They left you alone.
You sat, palms on the couch, four thousand
days behind you. That awkward

age: Was it harvest or spring? Still
nervous in the dark, already versed
in guilt. Waiting to be chewed, fried,

gunned down, stabbed. The horizon flew
at you, ripe wheat advancing, golden
muskets cocked. You'd never gotten away

with anything. Lies. Curses. Prayers
for the disappearance of your parents: The dead
tree bared its alligator chops, flames

slithered through gyproc. No way
down from the porch. You jumped, they
succumbed. Now you prefer to be

alone in the tied-down house, with
your intentions, assemblies of demons, blemishes
pulsing, warty feet shrieking

in their hinges. Harvest closes in. You
don't know if you would run
to Mali or Brazil. Strangle the thing

that presses you into the couch (if only
you could see it.) Breathe. Confront
the sharpened air, that tuber hope, nestled

in unplowed rows. Windows blink. Lemony
tulips open briefly. There are three
chimneys by which to plot your escape.

BADGES SEWN BENEATH EYEBALLS

After *Elizabeth and I*, 1931, André Kertèsz,
gelatin silver print

I know, as surely as the hot material
of my dress crumples in the sweating, pinching
place beneath my arms: There is more to life
than this. There is more than a muscled

arm flung over my shoulder to warn me: stay
put. There is more than this satin fringe to conceal
my ankles. There must be more than that bland
striped tie I watch you twist into shape

each morning, and unwind into crumpled ribbon
the nights you come home. The difficulty lies
in knowing it exists, but neither how nor where
to acquire this missing piece. What is one to do

but pose? Cross legs, draw knees in, toward
the chest. Wear hair tied so it tugs
at the cheeks, and black smudges shading
the eyes as though they portend nothing

that couldn't be found in the dark
corner of a room, if you dared to look. Badges
sewn beneath eyeballs, they declare: may it all
go on. Let it whip at my pocked skin,

flattened brow. Cameras click, hot flashes
striking. I will not blink. I will not bother
to fit into the crook of your arm. I will wind
my square-faced watch and fasten my lips.

TRAVEL PHOTOS

I am trucker, I am
the son-of-a-bitch you thank,
ought to, every day, you:

gnawing gristle, zipping jeans, sucking
back that whiskey sizzle, gold
plating your throat. My motto: You got it,

some baggy-eyed trucker brought it: leaky
watermelon, booze, tubes of goop. I,
trucker, don't be thinking fucker, so

it rhymes, so what. Driver with cramped
legs, yanking my horn for the school bus,
soaking into leather, breathing out

the back. My turf: Potholes, the sky-hole,
this metal tent crouched over rubber planets hurtling
whooeee—down two-lane nights. Peeling off

one mile at a time. You think it's fun, the Trans-Canada
slog through New Nowhere? Crumbling
tar, rotting shoulders, looming from every

curve: the chance to career, to skid. You and your
pulsing dash, fifty-inch setback axle, goddamn
giant potatoes in your path, nickels up north

and Easter eggs wobbling over plains, down
some prickle-pine valley past a road-kill
skunk. I dream with eyes propped, edges

closing in, double-yellow warnings
racing all the way to God. I am hauled
from behind the wheel by the world's largest

fly rod; tip toy cows, big immobile fuckers
with Kodak smiles, their paint-chipped flanks
crashing into traffic, falling east now.

Send the kids postcards from Stickney,
from Pokiok, Sackville, Petitcodiac: any place
with a name worth a stamp, any place I've pitched

my steel tent, anywhere I've stopped to piss, eat
scrambled grease, with ketchup, click
the shutter. Tonight. A woman

in wildcat fur, camel heels, mauve
dusk stroking my orange-brandy
cab. Never wanted her, just

the brash pink of her on my
cooling cab—hints of meadow-valley
nirvanas. I am chauffeur, harbour Buddhist

leanings: One coffee, one picture per
stop. Me, trucker, motor humming, breathing in time
to her glassy photo rocking back and

forth. My boredom, her thighs. Take
the wildcat woman to Cabano, maybe Jemseg. Cross
to Mars Hill, Maine, somewhere. Free her

from the mirror, window down, wind
rejoicing. Nothing wrong with torn-up
mauve and a narrow road, load scattered in sun,

off a bridge, rinsing pine-needle hills.

GAS BAR BOY

Through the gas bar. See him
lean, Pepsi machine for a wall,
ember rising, lips waiting, cap

just so. As if he deserves
to star in this concrete scene. As if
he owns that vintage Ford, its silver-rail

bumper, body washed with wine. It crouches
in the garage: sour, enduring—
with feline airs. Would he sell

his future for a spin? Some day he may care
as little as he desires. He slouches
under youth's accusations, threatening

to pounce. The past lies mutely
along the creases of his jeans.

BILLBOARD GIRL

Clouds, strands of dust, threads
of grey on smoke-blue sky, wish
to stay put. But a flower-petal fan clicks,

whirrs, urges them past the billboard
girl in goggles who dreams (we suppose)
of white, sliced bread. She's slapped

on the broad haze like a stamp, yet all who pass
beneath feel small. Evergreens scratch
library brick. The edge is a tiring place to be.

Cape Breton Relative

CHAPTER I

In Which You Approach from the Northwest, by Car, over a Rise

Wheels black and racing hear that red spruce scolding:
Jesus Murphy b'y! When were you last down home?
The island with her prickly thighs. Her porkpie mouth.
She is your Aunt Mavis. She wants to know where you've been.

Jesus Murphy b'y, when you were last down home!
From the Big Stop regard her pebbly arm, yellowed vein.
She is your Aunt Mavis, wants to know: where you've been,
how many causeways in the world, limbs to pull you ashore?

From the Big Stop regard her pebbly arm, yellowed vein
dividing the faithful, departing. Pay her toll, dear, knowing
how few causeways in the world, limbs to pull you ashore,
sloshed right and left by tides, reeling in,

divining the faithful departing. Pay her dear toll knowing
she is old, blood involved, will forget you're barely more than a tourist
right sloshed by tides, left reeling in
your smog-bitten face, highrise eyes.

She is old blood, involved will. Forget you're barely more than a tourist
in her beery, seawater throat. She kisses and kicks
your smog-bitten face, highrise eyes
in which cities dissolve as you broach her, fiddles weeping

in her beery, seawater throat. She kisses and kicks
you, fed up with love, those sharp little bites.
Cities dissolve as you broach her, fiddles weeping
though none of your relatives play. No kitchen parties

for you, fed up with love, those sharp little bites
tormenting off shore. Were you better off in Ontario?
Though none of your relatives play (no kitchen parties)
blare across the Causeway, your hearty salt reels

tormenting the shore. Were you better off? In Ontario
Aunt Mavis would be at a loss for words, boiling her tea.
Blare across the Causeway. Your salty heart reels,
wheels black and racing. Hear that red spruce scolding.

CHAPTER II

In Which You are Welcomed by Black Flies, Twenty-eight Brands of
Mosquito, and Children Who Jump Recklessly from Bridges

And water, cold and deep as prehistoric
joy. A Tim Horton's every hundred feet. Your whistling
uncle who calls you Shorty and Dora and Dummy. And the man

with the dog at the Mira Ferry Irving: doling
lollipops, selling gas. Main-à-dieu frogs spit their wet
hellos on your car. The house clumps into view.

Daisies, alders, three stumpy pines. Strawberries
sugar the air. Lace webs windows, trinkets creep
down walls—Nan's varnished Marys, sacred plastic

heart on a bitty wooden plaque—too polite to ask
why you drove all this way, where it is you're trying
to get. Stand atop the bank. Remember a black dog, Grampy's

limp, Nan's wrinkly Os of surprise. Those frogs in the pond
nearly drowned you, Dummy, when you were three. Hard
bites ring your neck. Your uncle in the fish plant cracking

legs off crab, ramming their brittle heads, hollowed
orange dwellings about his feet. In winter he'll carve
his meticulous faith: fire trucks, dolphins, swords. What'll it be,

for you? Kids on bridges gust into place, plastered
in short wet suits. You never meant to join their careless
leaping. Swim through the kitchen splashing old

prints onto walls. Your uncle whistles down at the new
cushion floor. Wring out a seat, two cups. Empty his
pail of jokes. Your shoulder in the door, eyes on the chair

where she ought to be sweetening her tea.

CHAPTER III

In Which You Give in to the Urge to Write Home

Tell him, you must, of wind in your shoe, of bats
and moths, babies tangled in your hair. Address him as dear. Remind him

fog and flight paths re-appear. Will he straighten his spine, summon
your missives with light in his eyes? Drink you down with a cold

ginger ale. Begin with the letter L. For longing, sloppily
ladled. Logic, la-la, lust. Latitudes of pain

separated by history, geography. Low-lying strata you never
discuss. Should he know about the three dogs converging on you

at dusk? Your jog interrupted. That night at the concert: beer in hand, clammy
ring of hope around your wrist. Silly codes like kite, and hat, and smooch. How

you scrambled your names into breakfast dishes, circled the planet
wielding expectation. Don't write that the camera has choked on yet another

picture of a clothesline. How many degrees of longitude shouldered
between you now? The bridge that refused to swing you through might be a sign

you don't want him to see. Pretend the island is secluded, its intentions
not clear. Read replies like a pilot prepped for turbulence. Choppy wind,
his name.

CHAPTER IV

In Which You Take Your Friend, Who Has Never Before Visited
Cape Breton, to the Tar Ponds in Sydney

It's not the whole tour, alright? She's seen the back
shore, its bleary eye on Mira Bay, cheekbone scarred in calcium
white: J&B were here. Heard browning ferns and newborn
spruce rehash burns, theories on black flies, failing

in love. Slapped that pop machine by the wharf, only
commerce since Mullins' store, thick with men
on vinyl chairs. Heard the yellowed weeping of wrecks
in the two-room museum, that famous woman's nosedive

into a bog at Baleine. The fire of '76 scalping hills, leaping
the road. That permed volunteer reading archival walls,
taking calls, so she'd know it all: The ambulance bawled
this morning for Mrs. L. with the water on the lungs

who refused to see her doctor when she ought. The seniors'
home, its improbable lawn of white crosses. Another cemetery
backing on the sea: Great-Uncle Vesty who drowned, all those infants
perishing the same few years. Moque Head where you raked

mussels with your string-bean uncle, ripping threads
from clutches of stone. The ballpark's fence of diamond oceans
where he played before the accident, before you knew about dark-haired
heroes, their mistakes. At the tar ponds she opens her mouth

to a truth that never arrives. You want to tell her you have held
the tar, rubbed its sheen: Life in steel was hard
but satisfying. As if you know. Who knows why
we make such messes to feed ourselves. This is our lot:

pits of blackness sealed in quiet
pools. Unfathomable love. Weather, fire. Endings
pressing into rock. The tender, smoke-stained gums of unknowable men.

CHAPTER V

In Which You Learn to Tell Them Your Father's Name Before They Ask

And the name of the beach that sprung
him, from rock: slick, lichened, corroded
even then. Buddy in the Lobster Kettle, young
thing at Value-Check unrolling floors, bloated
miner in the museum shaft holding his lung:
Feed it to them fast: He's a laah-he floated
down from Main-à-dieu. Words that get you
in: that reek of generations, crazy island glue.

That ritual bathing when you arrive: boil
away from your skin, let dampness in. Trudge
the graveyard heap sucking up soil,
mulch of your boned past. Letters budged
into granite, angled paths, dead ends all.
You are not what you are, anymore. How to nudge
truth from a name? Your father's father was a father
alright—but not, you have learned, his own. Why bother

trying to convince him rumours are all just
drama? French-Canadian soldier, war-time fling, his blood
shipping boldly out from Glace Bay. It is you who must
picture a rape behind the Savoy, cold mud
on your grandmother's easy-rip dress, that no-fuss
approach to making rags, moving on. Your father's head
a clue tightly worn. That tidy, mysterious jaw.
Think of him as residue. Bestow on him your awe.

There are things kept only in the gravel
of your bones, the white open palms of hips.
If you return to tombstones consider it travel:
Regard the dead coolly, as you would an unmarked ship.
We have all been mislabelled, packaged to baffle,
surprise. A name gives shape to the palest of lips:
James, Alice, Mary, Charles, George—trace
their stony, bloodless letters, this familial place.

CHAPTER VI

In Which You are Told, Once and for All, About Fishermen

Greedy lot. Always after complainin'.
Gossipers, oh my dear, if you heard them.
And tender—stay right at home when it's rainin'.
Three hundred grand: Imagine such a sum
for a month of lowering, hoisting. Them pining
for more. Couldn't smile either, sea might thumb
their arses. Never pleased, no joys.
Buncha sooks with fibreglass toys.

Greedy lot, they are. Always after bellowin'
the price of this, government that. Rough weather?
In the old days lobstermen drowned and kept rowing.
Now it's waterproof suits and GPS, feather
pillows, motors what shine. Whispers glowing
onscreen, a white cold pulse—together
they make the ocean talk: Rocks here. Sand there.
A rich man's traps come prepared.

You reckon they're windblown, muted
by the sea? Your grandfather was a superstitious
fart with Palm Sunday crosses in his bow who hated
to float, drank till three, till four, till the most vicious
rowing got him nowhere. His pilfered traps. Polluted
nights in his watery, try-try heart, cleaning dishes
no one was meant to catch. Times he fell gentle, kind as sin.
Whiskey, salt and guilt, it's them, what mar your kin.

CHAPTER VII

In Which You Jog Past Sites of Hardship, Honing Technique

Immaculate Conception Catholic Church: Iced
prettily. Drop your knees low, lower, low. Fling
forward, your leg on its hinge. Picture the steps

of the church that burnt down. Sunday: your father, his
brothers, waiting for the men to shrug inside, snatching
their red-ended butts from the dirt (how to smoke when you

can't afford shoes). Exhale, inhale. Breathe out, and out.
The hunkered school, mouths crammed with cores
and peels (all they got with a fisherman father

who slept till noon). That horn of plenty you drew, bowls
your mother filled and refilled. Loosen your wrists, quit hunching
as if you've got something to hide. The empty lot where he

lived: the ocean, the uncle on its shore, the gun in the hand
of the uncle on its shore, the bullet from the gun
in the hand of the uncle, running him down the shore

one bottomless night. Take it long; run it
slow. Shoulders back and low; hips up and out. The melting
at the edges of the earth reveals everything, nothing. The bullet

sand-lodged, burrowed, his mind, no
prying it out. You have forgotten your breathing, why
you are here. The boardwalk, stilted, going off

in all directions. Water clasps a woman's thighs. Her black dog
bares his teeth, then joins you, panting. Echoes of hammers, slat
after slat. Echoes of men who remember

work that wasn't just for show. The dog trundles
ahead, happy tongue leading the way. Feel the wood
absorb your heel, the memory it bears: kathunk, kathunk.

CHAPTER VIII

In Which Your Uncle Recalls the Last Time He Traversed
the Treacherous Tiddle on the Way to Scaterie

"Twelve, I was, and after duck. The boat
a dropped ladle, dipping, rolling, old George
steering, old George drunk, one-legged George:
his gun, his whiskey, his dog and full throat
of smoke against the froth, the belch: the tiddle
versus the hull. The day was yellow, mean.
At George's boots a can of gasoline,
puncture in its side: a greasy dribble.

"Imagine. Sure we landed, hunted. Fire
in my dreams? I don't suppose. I plucked
my dinner, dear. I guess you might admire
me for that." Old George, old times, old luck.
Your uncle laughs and veers toward the rock.
Your uncle drinks; the bottom splashes higher.

CHAPTER IX

In Which You Visit Ruins, Seals, and the Automated Light at Scaterie

Imagine Nan among wild dogs, alders, weather.
One dirt road, one dirt path. An island off an island:
ten kilometres long, three wide. From here to Scotland,
nothing but waves. You are walking to the light:

one dirt road, one dirt path. An island off an island.
The people, when they lived here, chose the far side—
nothing but waves, you, walking to the light,
four of you strung like jigs on a line, snagged ghosts

of the people who lived here, chose the far side.
Two houses remain: on the point, by the light.
Four of you strung—jigs on a line, snagged ghosts—
in thick green netting that hugs the rock, holds it together.

Two houses remain on the point. By the light,
seals wag their noses, buoys in the surf barking warnings
as thick green netting hugs the rock, holds it together.
A rabbit on the road. Sun palming your back.

Seals wag their noses, buoys in the surf barking warnings
at you, poised on a rotting beam, wide-eyed:
a rabbit on the road, sun palming your back,
shards at your ankles. Nan's lips pursed

at you, poised, the rotting beam. Wide-eyed
glass once tamed this sky, cut it into squares.
Shards at your ankles, Nan's lips pursed,
amused at your reaction. You walk to the light wishing

to tame the sky, cut it into squares,
to bless the seal carcass: fetal, frail. Four nameless graves,
amused at your reaction. You walk to the light wishing
to free traps twined with weeds, unroll the storms that flung them here.

Bless the seal carcass, fetal, frail. Four nameless graves
erect on a swell of land, clammy with regret.
Free traps twined with weeds, unroll the storms that won here,
fill the doorway. This empty house: see how it dies

erect on a swell of land, clammy with regret
ten kilometres long, three wide, here to Scotland.
Fill the doorway, this empty house. See it die.
Imagine Nan among wild dogs, alders, weather.

CHAPTER X

In Which a Pair of British Tourists Board a Propeller Plane in Halifax

And believe it will fly them to Australia. You read this
over breakfast at Jasper's: poached eggs, brown toast. Saturday.
Six days left on the island, on your own. The lost travellers

sit bag-eyed on the front page of the *Cape Breton Post*, patchy
airport grass flattened beneath their bums, a sunny
Air Canada employee propped nearby on hefty,

motherly arms. Will their carelessness save her
from some ordinary despair? You wish someone could
hear you laugh, someone you love. The week progresses. Run,

read, line the window with yellow rocks, tell yourself
I was here. Reporters call from London, Berlin, to investigate
disappointment: landing in the Sydney without

the opera house. The mayor declares we have all been insulted
by the BBC. The couple is seen in the Mayflower Mall, Sobey's,
the lobby of the Holiday Inn. They are 19, don't drive—you despise

yourself but keep reading. The airline employee drives them
to the Fortress. They shrug off our ageing
stone: Their country is full of it, bald, grey and rolling

out of walls. You are supposed to be mending
heartache, touring back to your own wrong turn. You crave
accidental deliverance. No maps, none of that agitating

hope. It's no good. There's always some local
to show you around, ruin your chances of staying
lost. The Brits fly home. A reporter writes *No,*

the flight is not to London, Ontario. Laugh softly, lonesomeness
smudging your fingertips, staining your arm.

CHAPTER XI

In Which a Teenage Boy Sings a Lament to Tourists at Louisbourg

His voice peers from behind curls, lit
before the crowd. His face white as the arch
of your foot, and as tender. The song
is popular, he says (with disappointment). He'll
sing it the way it was made: with boiled tears, failure
of the tide receding. He shuts his eyes, you

disappear. He has not yet known
love, only these notes, the words that rest
upon them, gifts he opens in his throat. The song:
a farewell older than the boy. He summons a future
sorrow to his tongue, holds it there, breathing. It rises
over bowed heads, a dissolving caress, all the ones you have lost.

CHAPTER XII

*In Which Your Cousin Unravels a Tangled Line in Preparation
for Jigging Mackerel Off the Shore at Scaterie*

You could watch him till your death
in the muttering boat, circling
thin blue line over and into itself. He bends,
an upturned L nosing through snags
into wonders, all the wounds

in your twist-tied heart that might never
recover its own beginnings, balled-up
ends. He peels his way into knots, stands
them down: tasks you simply
do, on water, gulls on your tail, tide

slinking out. See him cradle
the problem beneath his chest
so it won't get away. Winds, invisible
salts, envelop his whispering
hands that tie and untie, trailing

rescued coils along the deck. Scales
lift off your face, the bitten
base of your neck. How easily a man will take
you apart, put you back together (or
not). Your cousin warns you this way, teasing

air through that wild blue mess. Does he know
what he's saying? His is the face you wore
when you wished you were a boy, immune
to the tangles of girlishness. He had
skills you knew you'd never acquire. In a moment

he will look your way, smile, everything
unwound. O, that the future would heap so cleanly
by the feet. Think of his wife, their new boy,
lives you will and will not lead. How many

fish will clamber to their shiny, sharp-edged doom, redden
blue curls of paint in the bottom of the boat.

CHAPTER XIII

In Which You Attempt to Jig Mackerel, Then to Cut
Them Up in a Process Known as "Cleaning"

Your job: to wipe out a school without
mangling a thumb on baubles that crook and snake
into fish-mouths, skin, whatever lets them in. When in doubt
keep lowering your prongs. These fish aren't afraid
of the dark. They'll tug when they want to come out.
They rise in threes, panting through eyeballs, opaque.
Your father once told you fish weren't cursed with nerves:
"What a creature doesn't feel, it deserves."

Once a fish is on a hook, it might refuse
to let go. Adopting the pose of the faithful
it hangs by one lip, deflecting light. You yank & lose
hold—your flapping mouth. This facial
reduction before the kill. Mackerel don't sing the blues.
They bleed and pelt the thighs of the boat, its palatial
gut. How ordinary, quick, this staining of the pail,
this weighing of bodies, scalping of scales.

Your uncle hacks through all but one before you summon
the nerve to try it yourself. The blade extends
from your hand; it hears a taunting: please, come in.
One cut, back of the gills. Turn the knife. Now. Rend
flesh from bone, ease into a state of filet, fresh lemon
sharpness numbing your tongue. The thrown carcass intends
to lie tragically on a wave, sending a skeletal moan
into the sea that gave it up. Your dripping hands; a seagull drone.

CHAPTER XIV

In Which You Skim the Surface of the Mira

The river doesn't scold. She is molten, spiralled with the oily
mauves of dusk. She lets you pass, easing into endless
folds. She calls her bats to perform their aerial tricks, reunites

their flung bodies with the sky, its thousand hands, released
from dank corridors under rock. The river carries her gifts without
caring who will earn them. Eels and boats. Jellyfish, children. Ageing

dogs bound into her, splash her over docks. She permits
weeds to be dredged from her guts, where coldness and warmth
bump one another like feverish wrecks. In the morning

she holds your pink feet, takes pity on you, the way
you have hardened in some places, softened in others.

CHAPTER XV

In Which You Wander the Island, Pondering Geography

With him you belong
any old place: faraway cliff-top
blue in his eyes, grassy hollows
warmed into his chest. You climb

daily into that crevice
below his jaw, survey the jagged,
sculpted world. It matters not
what you see, you see it round-eyed,

blessed. Prepare, even now. This nook
will fill in: avalanche, dust, some squatter
who follows you scrambling into love
one tired old night. Without his muscular

laughter, thighs and plains, list
your criteria for home:
berries underfoot or a bird-sized
pocket in which to furl, high

above teeming streets? Will you tramp
through swampy yards or claw
your way into clouds, from one wobbling
sphere to another? Will you at last lose

him, or recover yourself? It comes down
to liquid crossings, glass in dappled
sheets. Salt clumping pores, rivers circling
ankles. White gashes

in the sky, through which only you will fit.

Notes

Several poems in this book, aside from those that appear with subtitles, were also born through contemplation of particular works of visual art.

The figure in "Woman at Clothes Line" was drawn from a painting of the same title by Alex Colville (1957, oil on masonite).

"A Woman to Her Abdomen, Hanging on the Line" takes its central image from the work *Thanksgiving* (1985), by Jane Martin.

"Wash Day in a Toronto Slum" is based on a photograph from the City of Toronto Archives titled "Dept. of Health photo 315. August 27, 1914. Front St. Rear 512."

"The Usual Spin" was instigated by a photograph of Alexander Lahey by Mark Sutcliffe.

"The Element of Carrying On" was written during a windy shift as a volunteer at the Main-à-dieu Fishermen's Museum on Cape Breton Island, and inspired in part by the miniature fishing boats on display, built by William Keeping.

"Gasping" is based on a photo from Lourdes, Nfld., by William DeKay that appeared in *Canadian Geographic* (Through the Lens, 1998).

"Consumption" speaks to the painting *Hunger* by Rudolph Schlichter.

"High Diver" is in response to a print of the same title by Alex Colville (1957).

"Convictions, at Fourteen" relates to the painting *Ludivine* (c. 1930), by Edwin Holgate.

"No One Watching" was written after the painting *Ontario Farmhouse* (1934) by Carl Schaefer.

"Travel Photos" was imagined based on the painting *Western Star* by Alex Colville (1985).

Carmine Starnino, Editor
Michael Harris, Founding Editor

SELECTED POEMS David Solway
THE MULBERRY MEN David Solway
A SLOW LIGHT Ross Leckie
NIGHT LETTERS Bill Furey
COMPLICITY Susan Glickman
A NUN'S DIARY Ann Diamond
CAVALIER IN A ROUNDHEAD SCHOOL Errol MacDonald
VEILED COUNTRIES/LIVES Marie-Claire Blais (Translated by Michael Harris)
BLIND PAINTING Robert Melançon (Translated by Philip Stratford)
SMALL HORSES & INTIMATE BEASTS Michel Garneau
    (Translated by Robert McGee)
IN TRANSIT Michael Harris
THE FABULOUS DISGUISE OF OURSELVES Jan Conn
ASHBOURN John Reibetanz
THE POWER TO MOVE Susan Glickman
MAGELLAN'S CLOUDS Robert Allen
MODERN MARRIAGE David Solway
K. IN LOVE Don Coles
THE INVISIBLE MOON Carla Hartsfield
ALONG THE ROAD FROM EDEN George Ellenbogen
DUNINO Stephen Scobie
KINETIC MUSTACHE Arthur Clark
RUE SAINTE FAMILLE Charlotte Hussey
HENRY MOORE'S SHEEP Susan Glickman
SOUTH OF THE TUDO BEM CAFÉ Jan Conn
THE INVENTION OF HONEY Ricardo Sternberg
EVENINGS AT LOOSE ENDS Gérald Godin (Translated by Judith Cowan)
THE PROVING GROUNDS Rhea Tregebov
LITTLE BIRD Don Coles
HOMETOWN Laura Lush
FORTRESS OF CHAIRS Elisabeth Harvor
NEW & SELECTED POEMS Michael Harris
BEDROCK David Solway
TERRORIST LETTERS Ann Diamond
THE SIGNAL ANTHOLOGY Edited by Michael Harris
MURMUR OF THE STARS: SELECTED SHORTER POEMS Peter Dale Scott
WHAT DANTE DID WITH LOSS Jan Conn
MORNING WATCH John Reibetanz

3 1817 01334 5434

JOY IS NOT MY PROFESSION Muhammad al-Maghut
(Translated by John Asfour and Alison Burch)
WRESTLING WITH ANGELS: SELECTED POEMS Doug Beardsley
HIDE & SEEK Susan Glickman
MAPPING THE CHAOS Rhea Tregebov
FIRE NEVER SLEEPS Carla Hartsfield
THE RHINO GATE POEMS George Ellenbogen
SHADOW CABINET Richard Sanger
MAP OF DREAMS Ricardo Sternberg
THE NEW WORLD Carmine Starnino
THE LONG COLD GREEN EVENINGS OF SPRING Elisabeth Harvor
FAULT LINE Laura Lush
WHITE STONE: THE ALICE POEMS Stephanie Bolster
KEEP IT ALL Yves Boisvert (Translated by Judith Cowan)
THE GREEN ALEMBIC Louise Fabiani
THE ISLAND IN WINTER Terence Young
A TINKERS' PICNIC Peter Richardson
SARACEN ISLAND: THE POEMS OF ANDREAS KARAVIS David Solway
BEAUTIES ON MAD RIVER: SELECTED AND NEW POEMS Jan Conn
WIND AND ROOT Brent MacLaine
HISTORIES Andrew Steinmetz
ARABY Eric Ormsby
WORDS THAT WALK IN THE NIGHT Pierre Morency
(Translated by Lissa Cowan and René Brisebois)
A PICNIC ON ICE: SELECTED POEMS Matthew Sweeney
HELIX: NEW AND SELECTED POEMS John Steffler
HERESIES: THE COMPLETE POEMS OF ANNE WILKINSON, 1924-1961
Edited by Dean Irvine
CALLING HOME Richard Sanger
FIELDER'S CHOICE Elise Partridge
MERRYBEGOT Mary Dalton
MOUNTAIN TEA Peter Van Toorn
AN ABC OF BELLY WORK Peter Richardson
RUNNING IN PROSPECT CEMETERY Susan Glickman
MIRABEL Pierre Nepveu (Translated by Judith Cowan)
POSTSCRIPT Geoffrey Cook
STANDING WAVE Robert Allen
THERE, THERE Patrick Warner
HOW WE ALL SWIFTLY: THE FIRST SIX BOOKS Don Coles
THE NEW CANON: AN ANTHOLOGY OF CANADIAN POETRY
edited by Carmine Starnino
OUT TO DRY IN CAPE BRETON Anita Lahey

Véhicule Press

THELMA FANNING MEMORIAL
LIBRARY NANTON

JAN 2 1 2008